THE BERMUDA TRIANGLE

BY
JIM COLLINS

A

Book

RSVP
RAINTREE
STECK-VAUGHN
PUBLISHERS
The Steck-Vaughn Company

Austin, Texas

First Steck-Vaughn Edition 1992

Copyright © 1977 Contemporary Perspectives, Inc.

Art and Photo Credits

Cover illustrations by Lynn Sweat.
Photos on pages 7, 23, 26, 28, 42 and 47, United Press International.
Illustrations on pages 9, 15, 20, 34 and 35, James Warhola.
Map on page 11, Alfred Fusco.
Photos on pages 18 and 39, "The Bermuda Triangle"—Berlitz, courtesy of J.M. Valentine.
Photo on page 29 and illustration on page 30, Culver Pictures, Inc.
Photo on page 44, J.H. Golden/Photo Researchers, Inc.
All photo research for this book was provided by Roberta Guerrette.
Every effort has been made to trace the ownership of all copyrighted material in this book and to obtain permission for its use.

Library of Congress Number: 77-21808
Library of Congress Cataloging in Publication Data

Collins, Jim.
    The Bermuda triangle.

    SUMMARY: Discusses the many mysterious, unexplained losses of ships and planes in the area of the Atlantic Ocean between Florida and Bermuda.
    1. Bermuda Triangle—Juvenile literature.
[1. Bermuda Triangle] I. Title.
G558.C64   001.9′4   77-21808

ISBN 0-8172-1050-4 hardcover library binding

ISBN 0-8114-6851-8 softcover binding

22 23 24 25 26   96 95 94 93 92

CONTENTS

Chapter

1

FLIGHT 19
IS MISSING!

It was a clear spring-like day in Fort Lauderdale, Florida. The time was December 5, 1945. The day was calm and cloudless. Only a light wind was blowing from the northeast—perfect weather for flying.

World War II was over. America was slowly returning to a more normal life. But on this day something very strange was to happen. At first, the mystery would hardly be noticed. Later, only a few questions would be raised. But, within 30 years, many would call this event the "most mysterious in the history of flying." What happened would be the first in a long chain of events in the mystery of the *Bermuda Triangle*.

Lieutenant Charles Taylor of the United States Navy was used to being a flight leader. He had over 2,500 hours of flying time to his credit. That December day Taylor was given command of Flight 19. The job seemed very simple. Five Avenger bombers were to go on a training flight. The five planes would carry a crew of 14.

Normally, there would have been 15 in the crew. But Corporal Allan Kosnar did not report for the flight. He had asked not to go on this mission. He received permission to stay on the ground. Later, Corporal Kosnar would say, "I can't explain why. But for some strange reason I decided not to go on the flight that day." Had Corporal Kosnar been warned? Had he known what was going to happen?

Lieutenant Taylor had also asked not to go on this flight. Permission had been denied. Had Taylor also been warned?

The Flight 19 record, however, reported a full crew. Mysteriously, it recorded 15 flyers. Had someone climbed aboard at the last minute?

Who was this person? Or was the report of 15 flyers just a mistake?

The flight was to take about two hours. Each plane had enough fuel for 1,000 miles. A careful check of all the planes was made before take-off. Life rafts were placed on board. The flyers were prepared for all emergencies. *Or were they?*

At 2 P.M., the first plane lifted off into the clear, blue sky. By 2:10 P.M., all of the planes were in the air. At first everything went well.

Five Avenger bombers took off on a training flight from Florida and were never seen again.

But then, about one and one-half hours into the trip, something happened. To this day, we cannot explain what it was. At around 3:45 P.M., the radio at the air station in Fort Lauderdale received this strange message from Flight 19:

Lieutenant Taylor: Calling tower. This is an emergency. We seem to be off course. We cannot see land. Repeat. We cannot see land.
Tower: What is your position?
Lieutenant Taylor: We are not sure of our position. We cannot be sure just where we are . . . We seem to be lost . . .
Tower: Assume bearing due west.
Lieutenant Taylor: We don't know which way is west. Everything is wrong . . . strange . . . We can't be sure of any direction—even the ocean doesn't look as it should.

Flight 19 was lost. Their compasses had gone crazy. Even the ocean didn't look familiar. All direction had been lost.

The naval base picked up conversations between pilots, but the tower could no longer reach the planes by radio. Soon, there was no sign of the planes on the radar screen. What had happened to Flight 19?

At 4:00 P.M., the tower crew heard Taylor turn over the command of Flight 19 to another pilot, Captain Stiver. Why?

The five planes stayed together. Captain Stiver reported they all seemed to be lost. For hours the planes flew aimlessly in all directions. Then, the very last words of Flight 19 came through. "It looks like we are . . . " The message was never completed. Some of the tower crew

The control tower tried frantically to contact Flight 19, but no message could reach them.

reported hearing one further message, "Entering white water . . . We are completely lost."

On the ground, emergency steps were immediately taken. A number of rescue planes were sent up after Flight 19. One was a giant Martin Mariner seaplane with a crew of 13. Soon a report of high winds came from the seaplane. Then no more reports came in. All radio contact was lost. *The rescue plane had vanished too!*

No more messages came from Flight 19 or the rescue plane except for one radio signal that evening. Shortly after 7:00 P.M., the tower at the Miami Naval Air Base heard "FT . . . FT . . . ," repeated very faintly. "FT" were two of the radio call letters of Flight 19. If that message came from Flight 19, it was sent *two hours after the planes would have run out of fuel.* Was it possible that Flight 19 could still be in the air?

The navy moved quickly into action. More rescue planes, joined by Coast Guard ships, were sent into the area. For the next few hours, and most of the following day, over 240 planes and 18 ships combed the area. Hour after hour, hundreds of eyes searched more than 280,000 square miles of sea and sky.

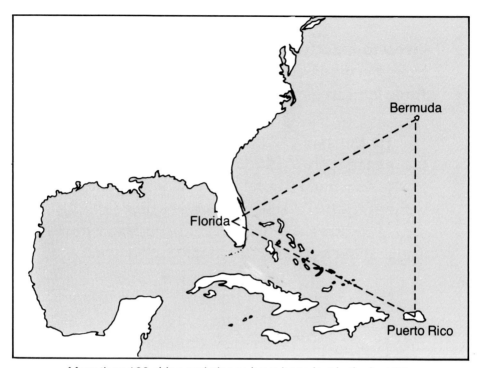

More than 100 ships and planes have been lost in the last 30 years in the area between Florida, Puerto Rico, and Bermuda. This area is the Bermuda Triangle.

No trace of the lost planes has ever been found. The navy has had official investigations of the mystery. They gathered every possible clue. Every piece of information has been examined. Their answer has never changed—*the planes seem to have vanished into thin air.* As one navy officer put it, "We are not even able to make a good *guess* as to what happened."

The loss of Flight 19 is only one of the famous mysteries of the *Bermuda Triangle*—the name

11

given to a part of the Atlantic Ocean that runs from Bermuda to Florida to Puerto Rico. The three land areas make up the "Triangle."

In the past 30 years, over 100 ships and planes and more than 1,000 people have been lost in the Bermuda Triangle. Most have vanished without trace. They have flown or sailed into this area of mystery and have never been heard from again. What happened to them?

To some people, Flight 19's disappearance in the Triangle is not mysterious at all. They feel that Lieutenant Taylor may simply have lost his bearings. He led his group off in the wrong direction. The planes, now flying off their course, ran out of fuel and crashed into the sea. The search effort may have been started too late. Maybe the area was too large to search carefully. Of course, this *could* account for the five planes of Flight 19. There is nothing said, however, about the Martin rescue plane and *its* disappearance.

There are people who say that the missing ships and planes in the Bermuda Triangle were gobbled up by flying saucers. Creatures from outer space have kidnapped earth men and women traveling through the Triangle to study what we are like.

While there are many people who believe there is something very strange about the Bermuda Triangle, there seems to be no agreement about what it is. Some say the laws of nature become "mixed up" in the Bermuda Triangle. These people believe the lost ships and planes have been sent into a different period of time. No one knows whether this time is in the past or future.

There are almost as many explanations as there have been disappearances. Some explanations are simple; others are far out. One thing is certain, however—people continue to disappear in the Bermuda Triangle.

Chapter

2

CHRISTOPHER COLUMBUS IN THE BERMUDA TRIANGLE

The mystery of the Bermuda Triangle goes back almost 500 years. As far as we know, Christopher Columbus, on his famous voyage in 1492, was the first to wonder about the strangeness of the Bermuda Triangle.

Part of the *Sargasso Sea* lies within the boundaries of the Bermuda Triangle. The Sargasso Sea is part of the Atlantic Ocean, with less wind, rain, and clouds than the rest of the ocean. Huge masses of seaweed cover the ocean floor in this area. Sailors passing over describe it as a gigantic jungle beneath the ocean.

Columbus' crew aboard the Santa Maria wanted to turn back
when the ship sailed through this strange part of the sea.

To add to the strangeness of this area, the Sargasso Sea is often so calm it is more like a lake than an ocean. Sometimes there is only a hint of a breeze. The water is very still. Many old sailors' tales tell of giant seaweed tangling around passing ships. The sailors, unable to breathe for lack of air, choked to death.

It is no wonder then, that the crew of the *Santa Maria* was terrified as it sailed, day after day, through this eerie stretch of sea. Columbus' crew grew so nervous they wanted to turn back.

But Columbus sailed on. Then something strange happened. It was the evening of September 13, 1492, a month before the discovery of America. The compass on the *Santa Maria* no longer pointed directly toward the North Star.

Instead, the compass needle pointed about six degrees northwest. The crew became upset. Sailors knew that they could count on the rising and setting of the sun, on the fixed positions of the stars, and on their compasses always pointing north. Their lives depended on such facts. The laws of nature seemed to have gone wild when they entered this area of the ocean.

It was hundreds of years after Columbus' voyage before the compass "mystery" could be explained. In the heart of the Bermuda Triangle, in the Sargasso Sea, compasses point directly true north. In almost every other area on earth, compasses point east or west of true north. They are actually pointing to the *magnetic north*–a few degrees east or west of true north. Though we now know what happened to Columbus' compass, his sailors had no way of knowing the difference between true and magnetic north.

Columbus was in for more mystery before he left the Bermuda Triangle. His ship's log reported that one night a great flame of fire shot across the sky. Then, a huge bolt of light suddenly flared up. As quickly as it appeared, it seemed to disappear. Was it a huge meteor flashing through the heavens? *Or was it something else?*

On October 11, 1492, Columbus' crew reported another strange glowing in the sea. It was a patch of white water. Centuries later, another group of explorers saw the same white area. These explorers were the astronauts of *Apollo 12*. They reported seeing glowing white water from hundreds of miles away in space. The astronauts could not explain the strange light and the glowing water.

Aerial view of white waters off Orange Key which were seen by
Columbus and by the astronauts of Apollo 12.

From the earliest voyages down to this very
day, ships and planes have reported strange hap-
penings in this patch of ocean called the Bermuda
Triangle. Of course, sailors have always told tall
tales of mystery and monsters. Maybe the
Bermuda Triangle has become one of these
legends of the sea. But how do we explain the
disappearances of ships and planes?

Chapter

3

IS THERE A "HOLE IN THE SEA"?

There have been many ships mysteriously lost within the waters of the Bermuda Triangle. Many other ships have been found without their original passengers. But lost ships and ship-wrecks are common. Why are the losses in the Bermuda Triangle mysterious? There are two major reasons. First, no trace of any of the lost ships has ever been found—no wreckage, no life rafts, and no bodies. Second, if the ship has been found, it appears to be in good condition. But it has become a *ghost ship*! The crew has disap-peared without a trace.

The most famous ghost ship is the *Mary Celeste*. It was found drifting just beyond the western limits of the Bermuda Triangle. On December 4, 1872, Captain David Morehouse of the *Dei Gratia* sighted the *Mary Celeste*. The sails were set and the sea was calm, but the ship seemed to be in trouble. Captain Morehouse sent a crew to investigate.

The *Mary Celeste* was a 103-foot brigantine weighing 282 tons. It had left New York a month

The *Mary Celeste*, a 19th century Brigantine was found adrift—a month after it left New York.

earlier. The ship carried a cargo of 1,700 barrels of alcohol. It also carried ten people, including the ship's captain, his wife, and baby daughter.

When the crew of the *Dei Gratia* reached the *Mary Celeste*, they found no one aboard. The ship did not appear to be damaged in any way. The cargo was still in place. Even the food supply was untouched. Money, pipes, and other personal objects had been left. Toys were found on the captain's bed as if he had been playing with his baby.

The captain's log book was also found, but it contained no record of trouble on the trip. The ship appeared to be normal in every way but one. All of the people on board were missing! Where were the passengers of the *Mary Celeste?*

There were many explanations. Some say a sudden tornado might have struck. (But why was the ship not damaged?) Some say pirates boarded the ship. (But why was the cargo left?) Some say the crew murdered the captain and his family. (Where did the crew go? And why was there no sign of struggle?) It was even said that Captain Morehouse boarded the ship and killed the crew. (Then why did he report the ship anyway?)

The case of the *Mary Celeste* has never been solved. For now, this ship seems to be just another victim of the Bermuda Triangle.

The *Mary Celeste* may be the most famous ghost ship, but the *Ellen Austin* is the strangest and most unbelievable. This case happened in 1881, nine years after the *Mary Celeste*.

Captain Baker of the *Ellen Austin* sighted a fine looking schooner sailing nearby. Because of the weather, it was a few days before the two ships were close enough to shout messages across. On August 20, Captain Baker tried to communicate with the drifting schooner. But there was no answer. So, the captain and four crewmen rowed over to the boat to investigate.

Baker found the ship to be in good condition. There was no sign of violence. There was a full supply of food and water. But again no one was aboard the ship. No crew, no captain. Not even a pet animal. The ship was searched from top to bottom. No trace of life was found. And there was no way to find out the name of the ship. The log book and the name plank were missing. It was another ghost ship afloat in the Bermuda Triangle!

A modern-day "ghost ship," the *Gloria Colita* was found in 1940 drifting in the waters of the Bermuda Triangle. There was no trace of its crew.

Under the laws of the sea, the ship now belonged to Captain Baker. Anything left abandoned on the high seas becomes the property of anyone who finds it. Captain Baker was confused but happy at his "good luck." He left part of his own crew aboard the ghost ship. Together, the two ships headed for Boston.

For two days all went well. Then, a sudden storm hit. For several days the winds raged, and the two ships lost sight of each other. The ghost ship was bounced away. Finally the storm passed. The sea was again calm. After some searching, the *Ellen Austin* sighted the other ship. It seemed intact, but Baker received no answer when he signaled. Again the captain and a few men boarded the ghost ship.

For a second time Baker found his ghost ship deserted. His own crew now had vanished without a trace. It almost seemed to Baker that they had never even been on board at all. The food had not been touched; the beds had not been slept in. And the new log book was missing. What had happened to the crew?

The captain was terrified. But he also wanted to keep his fine, new ship. At last, he persuaded some of his frightened crew to stay aboard the schooner. They were all fully armed. They were to stay within sight of the *Ellen Austin* at all times.

All went well for two days. Then they hit bad weather. There was no storm, but there was enough mist and rain that the two ships lost sight of each other for about 15 minutes.

The *Ellen Austin* went back to where the ghost ship was last seen. The crew of the *Ellen Austin* shouted, fired guns, and sounded their foghorn. There was no answer. They searched the entire area, but the ghost ship was nowhere to be found. Captain Baker had lost one third of his crew and his beautiful schooner. But to whom—or to *what*—had he lost them?

Another mysterious disappearance within the Bermuda Triangle occurred in 1918. The navy report of this case is one of the most frightening on record. The report covers the *U.S.S. Cyclops*—a big, 540-foot, 14,500-ton U.S. Navy fuel ship. The *Cyclops* was used to transport coal for the Navy.

In March, 1918, the *Cyclops* was moving from Barbados to Norfolk, Virginia. It carried a crew of 309 naval personnel and a full cargo. Its route took it through the Bermuda Triangle.

On March 13, 1918, the *Cyclops* was reported overdue at Norfolk. A search was launched for the missing ship. The *Cyclops* crew had a radio, but there had been no word of trouble from them. Thousands of miles of the ocean were searched. No trace of the ship was ever found. Anywhere else, such a disappearance would not be believed. In the Bermuda Triangle, however, it was becoming common for ships to simply vanish.

After President Woodrow Wilson read the *Cyclops* report, he said, "Only God and the sea know what happened to the great ship." But that did not stop many people from guessing at what happened to the *Cyclops*. Since America was at

The *Cyclops* completely disappeared in 1918, together with a naval crew of 309.

war with Germany at the time, it was first thought that the missing ship might have been torpedoed. No sign of wreckage was ever found.

In 1974, pieces of a shipwreck were found that might have come from the *Cyclops*. They could not be identified positively. As far as anyone knows to this time, the *Cyclops* simply vanished in the Bermuda Triangle.

Since the *Cyclops*, many ships, large and small, have been lost in the Bermuda Triangle. The loss of a large ship, of course, gets more attention. Such a ship was the *Marine Sulphur Queen*, lost in February, 1963.

A 523-foot tanker, the *Marine Sulphur Queen* was carrying a large crew and a cargo of sulphur. Routine radio messages were received giving the ship's position. But when they sailed into the waters of the Bermuda Triangle, the ship and its crew were never heard of again. A few life jackets were later found floating in the area, but they could not be identified as the ones on board.

Some people say the sulphur on board the *Marine Sulphur Queen* exploded. This caused the ship to sink. While this is possible, there was

Bound for Norfolk, Virginia in February, 1963, the *Marine Sulphur Queen* was another vessel that disappeared.

no sign of a ship explosion in the area. The case remains unsolved at this time.

The Bermuda Triangle also claimed one of the greatest sailors of all time. His name was Joshua Slocum. On April 24, 1895, at the age of 51, Slocum left Boston to begin a one-man journey around the world. Slocum sailed in a small, poorly equipped boat, the *Spray*. The *Spray* was less than 37 feet long. Slocum sailed the little boat on a 46,000-mile trip around the world. His adventure lasted three years. Slocum became the first man in history to sail around the world alone.

In 1909, Slocum set out on a one-man trip to the West Indies. In November, he stopped in Miami for supplies. Then he again headed out to sea. That was the last anyone heard of Joshua Slocum! Somewhere in the Bermuda Triangle, Slocum was lost. The man who had conquered

Joshua Slocum sailed around the world by himself in 1895. In 1909, he disappeared with his boat in the Bermuda Triangle.

the globe alone in a small boat had lost to the mysterious Bermuda Triangle.

Vanished ships, vanished crews, unexplained losses—*every case an unsolved mystery.* Explanations will be offered. Some may even be accepted. But the disappearance of ships within the Bermuda Triangle seems bound to continue.

The Spray, Joshua Slocum's 37 foot yawl, was claimed by the Bermuda Triangle in 1909.

Chapter

4

IS THERE A "HOLE IN THE SKY"?

Not only the sea within the Bermuda Triangle, but even the air above, is shrouded in mystery. In addition to ships, many planes have vanished in the Triangle. They appear to have been *snatched out of the sky.* Flight 19's disappearance was the most famous. Unfortunately, Flight 19 was not the only such air mystery over the Bermuda Triangle.

The case of two sister planes, the *Star Tiger* and the *Star Ariel,* is especially unusual. Both were passenger planes for British South American Airways. Each vanished in the month of

January—the *Star Ariel* was lost one year after the *Star Tiger*. Both vanished over the Bermuda Triangle.

The *Star Tiger* was on its way to Bermuda in the early morning hours of January 30, 1948. It carried 6 crewmen and 25 passengers. At 10:30 P.M., Captain Colby, pilot of the *Star Tiger*, radioed a routine message to a station in Bermuda. "Position approximately 400 miles northeast of you. Expect to arrive on time. Weather and performance excellent." Within minutes after that happy message, the *Star Tiger* was lost forever.

An effort to find the *Star Tiger* was led by Colonel Thomas Ferguson, commander of the U.S. Air Force Base in Bermuda. Although the missing plane was no longer in radio contact with the base, it still had enough fuel to last five hours. The weather was good and the water temperature was 65 degrees. If the plane had crashed into the sea, perhaps the crew had escaped.

Planes and ships searched the area for *Star Tiger* life rafts. Then, bad weather poured into the area. Not a radio signal from a raft, not a trace of the plane nor its passengers has ever been found. An official report of the search says, "What happened in this case will never be known." The disappearance of the *Star Tiger* is but one of the famous air mysteries in the Bermuda Triangle.

Almost exactly one year later *Star Tiger's* sister ship, the *Star Ariel*, was lost. The *Star Ariel* left Bermuda at 7:45 A.M., on January 17, 1949. Less than an hour later, Captain McPhee, the pilot, radioed this message to the tower in Bermuda: "We have reached cruising altitude. Fair weather. Expected time of arrival Kingston as scheduled . . ."

Those were the last words radioed from the doomed *Star Ariel*. Seven crewmen and 13 passengers were lost. No sign of the plane was ever found. The search for the *Star Ariel* was even bigger and longer than it had been for the *Star Tiger*. At one point, 72 search planes flew in a "wing tip to wing tip" pattern. They covered 150,000 square miles in their search but found nothing. Again the official report said, "Cause unknown."

Between the twin air disasters of *Star Tiger* and *Star Ariel* there was another plane lost—a DC-3 passenger plane.

Over 70 search planes were dispatched to look for the *Star Ariel*.
They found nothing.

The DC-3 was en route from Puerto Rico to Florida on December 28, 1948. It carried 36 people. The weather was fine and the night was clear. Pilot Robert Linquist radioed Miami during the night. He said, "What do you know? We're all singing Christmas carols!" Some hours later Linquist called in again. "We are approaching the field . . . 50 miles out . . . We can see the lights of Miami now. All's well. Will stand by for landing instructions."

When the radio tower in Miami tried to contact the DC-3, they got no answer. They continued calling to the plane, but the DC-3 was *gone*! It had disappeared within sight of the landing strip. No wreck, no bodies were ever found. It is especially strange that no SOS or call for help was ever heard from a plane so close to landing. Whatever happened to the DC-3, happened quickly. There was no time for a message.

In 1948, the pilot of a DC-3 reported seeing the lights of Miami. The plane with passengers and crew then disappeared without a trace.

In less than 12 months, 3 huge planes and 87 people vanished. A plane crash is a terrible thing, but usually it is not a mystery. A crash *does* become a mystery when there is no known reason for it. When a plane is lost and no trace of the wreck or bodies is ever found, we really have a mystery. When so many mysteries happen in one place, we can only be dealing with one of the world's great unsolved mysteries—the Bermuda Triangle.

Chapter

5

SURVIVORS OF THE TRIANGLE

The waters of the Bermuda Triangle are among the most traveled in the world. Thousands of planes, boats, and ships pass through the Triangle and nothing strange has happened to them. Others, as we have seen, are lost without explanation. Some lucky people met up with the strange forces in the Bermuda Triangle and lived to tell their stories.

Joe Talley was captain of a fishing boat called the *Wild Goose*. One night, Talley was on his own ship, asleep. Another boat, the *Caicos Trader* was towing the *Wild Goose* through the waters of the Bermuda Triangle. Suddenly, something strange happened. Water began to flood into the *Wild Goose,* drenching Talley. He woke up immediately and grabbed a life jacket, fighting for his life. Soon Talley was underwater.

The drowning captain somehow found the tow line and followed it up to the surface. He made it just in time. The *Caicos Trader* had to cut the line loose. Later, Talley was picked up by the *Caicos Trader.* It was then that Talley was told what had happened. Some "force" had hit the *Wild Goose,* pulling it underwater. The *Caicos Trader* had to cut loose so that it would not be pulled under, too. The *Wild Goose* had been lost, pulled down quickly and completely "as if in a whirlpool."

Joe Talley was one of the lucky ones. There have been other strange occurrences while boats were being towed through the Triangle. A Captain Henry tells one unusual story that happened to him in 1966. The captain, aboard the *Good News,* was towing an empty barge. It was afternoon. The weather was good, the sky was clear. Captain Henry was a confident, experienced man of the sea.

Suddenly the compass needle started spinning in circles. The sun was blotted out by low fog

This is the sister ship of the *Good News,* Captain Don Henry's ocean-going tug. Henry told of being in a "tug-of-war" while towing a barge through the Bermuda Triangle.

that quickly settled over everything. To Captain Henry, "The water, sky, and horizon all blended together. We couldn't see where we were."

Then something puzzling happened to the ship's electrical power. The generators seemed to be working. But there was no power on the boat.

Captain Henry was now worried about the barge he was towing. He couldn't see it. The barge seemed covered by a cloud. But the Captain remained calm. The line to the tow was still tight. Captain Henry tried to speed up the *Good News*. He wanted to get out of there quickly. But he felt something pulling him back. It was like a tug of war. After much struggle, Captain Henry finally won. The *Good News* and the barge came out of the fog or cloud.

Captain Henry recalled, "Have you ever felt two people pulling on your arms in opposite directions? It felt that we were on a place or point that somebody or something wanted. And somebody or something wanted us to be in another place from where we were going."

Others, too, have reported strange brushes with death in the Bermuda Triangle. They talk of odd things happening to their compasses and electricity. Some tell of fog banks or clouds that seem to suddenly cover the area. Sudden whirlpools form. Others talk of seeing strange lights in the sky. All of their stories do have one thing in common. *They are all glad to have escaped the Bermuda Triangle.*

Chapter
6

WHAT IS THE BERMUDA TRIANGLE?

You have read just some of the many reports of lost ships and planes in this strange area of the Atlantic called the Bermuda Triangle. These are neither stories of plane crashes nor shipwrecks. These are the cases of planes and ships that have completely vanished without a trace. They are the true reports of ships found in good condition, but with no sign of the crew. Can there be a reasonable explanation for these mysterious events?

Some people, including the United States Coast Guard, say the Bermuda Triangle *can* be explained. They feel every "mystery" reported

As recently as 1973, a 20,000-ton cargo ship, the *Anita,* and its crew of 32 were lost with no explanation.

has a natural cause. It's possible they are right. Those who believe the Triangle is an area of mystery say the others are mistaken. Those who believe there is a reasonable answer to the Triangle mystery make these points:

● The area of the Bermuda Triangle is one of the busiest waterways in the world. It is natural that more ships and planes are lost in such a busy area. One navy person says that "many,

many more disappearances" have happened in even busier shipping areas. They claim more ships are lost in the "Sable Triangle." This is an area that links Sable Island with the Azores and Iceland. They ask, "Why does no one talk of the *mystery* of the "Sable Triangle."

Those who believe in the Bermuda Triangle mystery say that navy officials have confused two different points. There may be more shipwrecks and plane crashes in the "Sable Triangle." But more ships, planes, and people have *simply vanished* in the Bermuda Triangle than anywhere else. These disappearances have never been explained.

• The naval people say that the lost planes and ships did not *vanish*. They were just not found. The ocean is very large. Lost ships and sailors are very hard to find when they are stranded at sea. It's like looking for a needle in a haystack.

The "mystery people" answer this by pointing out that the exact location of the lost ship or plane was known in almost every case. Even if the lost vessel was not found right away, some wreckage should have been found somewhere.

● The navy says the waters in the Bermuda Triangle are very dangerous. There are sudden storms lurking behind every cloud, ready to strike. The current of the Gulf Stream flows through the Bermuda Triangle. The area is likely to have sudden whirlpools or giant waves

Water spouts like this are often found off the coast of Bimini. They are sea tornadoes which can destroy objects in their direct path.

that roll without warning. Above the water, too, the air can be tricky. The area is noted for "clear air turbulence" (CAT). That means that flying conditions above the Triangle can change very quickly and without warning. One minute the sky is clear. The next minute some huge, powerful wind is sweeping the sky.

Believers in the strange powers of the Triangle agree with this explanation from the navy. The water and sky of the Bermuda Triangle are dangerous. Many of the lost pilots and sailors knew the area well. They knew the dangers. But many of the losses took place while the weather was fair. How can that explain the mysterious disappearances?

• The needle of a magnetic compass points to the magnetic north. But in a few places on earth the needle points to the true north, which can be several degrees east or west of magnetic north. The Bermuda Triangle is one of these places. That *could* account for the stories of crazy compasses. It *could* also account for many of the losses. The U.S. Coast Guard says, "If this compass *variation* is not [taken into account] a navigator could go far off course and into deep trouble."

Critics of the Coast Guard's explanation say most sailors and pilots know this strange fact about the Bermuda Triangle. They would have made the adjustment for compass variation.

Some people go so far as to say many of the stories about the Bermuda Triangle simply are not true. They feel that the strange reports are really "tales—the products of writers' imaginations." They even claim that the writers of Triangle reports hold back parts of the stories that would help explain the disappearances.

Certainly many stories have been made up by writers to add to the mystery of the Bermuda Triangle. But how do you explain Flight 19? Or the *Mary Celeste* incident? Or the *Star Tiger* and *Star Ariel?* For every such loss there must be some cause. Every missing ship or plane must be found. Every mystery has a reasonable explanation. Yet, in the mystery of the Bermuda Triangle, not a lost ship or plane has been found. Not one disappearance has a known cause. Not one strange report has been reasonably explained!

Finding the facts and figures in the Bermuda Triangle mystery is simple. In the last 30 years

One Florida boat owner tried locating his missing yacht by posting reward offers.

alone, more than 100 ships and planes and 1,000 lives have been lost. Finding the answers to the mystery of the Triangle, on the other hand, is not simple.

What happened to those who vanished in that area of the Atlantic known as the Bermuda Triangle? Is it possible we will never know?